LIVES
AND
TIMES

Pocahontas

Margaret Hudson

Heinemann Library
Chicago, Illinois

©2001 Reed Educational & Professional Publishing
Published by Heinemann Interactive Library,
an imprint of Reed Educational & Professional Publishing,
Chicago, Illinois

Customer Service 888-454-2279
Visit our website at www.heinemannlibrary.com

Designed by Ken Vail Graphic Design, Cambridge, England
Illustrations by Alice Englander
Printed in Hong Kong / China

03 02
10 9 8 7 6 5

Library of Congress Cataloging-in-Publication Data
Hudson, Margaret, 1955-
        Pocahontas / Margaret Hudson.
           p.   cm. — (Lives and times)
        Includes bibliographical references and index.
        Summary: A brief account of the life of the Indian princess who
befriended Captain John Smith and the English settlers of Jamestown.
        ISBN 1-57572-670-X (library binding)
        1. Pocahontas, d. 1617—Juvenile literature. 2. Powhatan women—
Biography—Juvenile literature. 3. Powhatan Indians—History—
Juvenile literature. 4. Jamestown (Va.)—History—Juvenile
literature. [1. Pocahontas, d. 1617. 2. Powhatan Indians—
Biography. 3. Indians of North America—Virginia—Biography.
4. Women—Biography.] I. Title. II. Series: Lives and times (Des
Plaines, Ill.)
E99.P85P57367 1998
975.5'01'092—dc21
        [B]   97-51457
                                                                        CIP
                                                                         AC

Acknowledgments
The Publishers would like to thank the following for permission to reproduce photographs: Ashmolean Museum p. 17;
Borough Council of King's Lynn and West Norfolk, courtesy of Mrs. Alex Stevenson p. 21; British Library p. 22; British
Museum pp. 18, 19; The Kobal Collection p. 23; National Portrait Gallery, Smithsonian Institute p. 20.

Cover photograph reproduced with permission of National Portrait Gallery.

Our thanks to Betty Root for her comments in the preparation of this book.

Some words are shown in bold, **like this**. You can find out what they mean
by looking in the glossary.

Contents

Part One

Pocahontas was born in about 1596, in what is now Virginia. She was a member of the Powhatan **tribe.** Her father was a chief. His name was Powhatan.

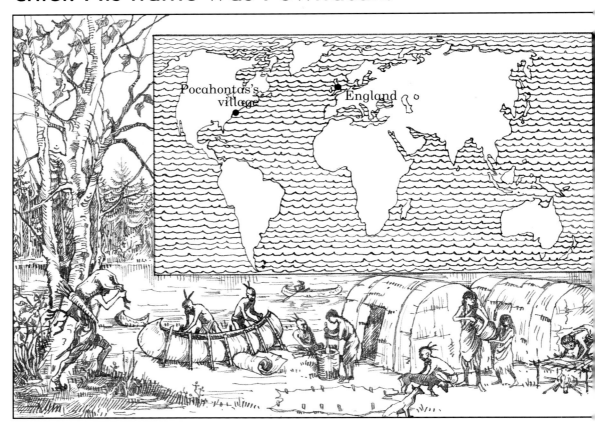

When Pocahontas was ten years old, explorers from England came to America looking for treasures. They built a small town called Jamestown near her village.

Pocahontas visited Jamestown and became friends with some of the English **settlers.** She taught them her language and they taught her English.

At first, the English and the Powhatan **tribe** were friendly. The settlers gave the Powhatan people tools and pots. In return, the tribe gave the English food.

The English wanted a lot of land to plant crops for food. The Powhatans also needed land to hunt and to farm. Soon the **settlers** and the **tribe** were fighting.

They did not always fight. During the winter, the English ran out of food and became sick. Pocahontas asked her father to send food to Jamestown, and he did.

Pocahontas and one Englishman, John Smith, were good friends. She became friends with him when she visited Jamestown. Some people believe a story that tells how she once saved his life.

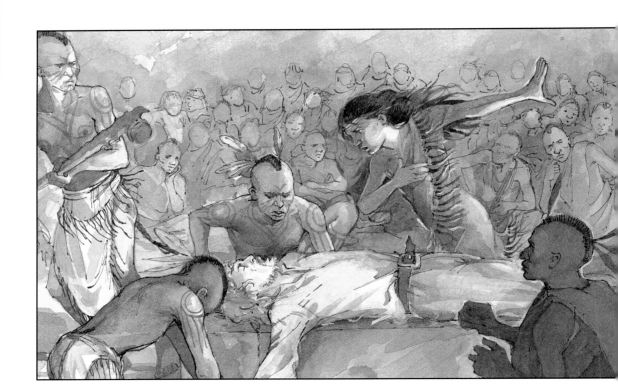

In this story, John Smith was caught by Chief Powhatan's **warriors.** The warriors wanted to kill John Smith because he was their enemy. Pocahontas saved his life by covering his body with hers.

When Pocahontas was about seventeen, she had to live in Jamestown. The **settlers** and the Powhatans hoped that this would stop them from fighting each other.

About a year later, in 1614, Pocahontas
married an Englishman named John Rolfe.
She was nineteen when she gave birth to
their son, Thomas. At last her father,
Powhatan, stopped fighting the English.

Pocahontas was now called Rebecca Rolfe.
In 1616, she left America to sail to England with
her husband and son. She met King James I and
many other important people.

Shortly before it was time to return to America, Pocahontas became ill. She died at Gravesend, England, before the ship sailed. She was only 21 years old.

Part Two

There are many **artifacts** from the time that tell us about Pocahontas and her life.

This **cloak** was made by the Powhatan people. It was sent by Chief Powhatan to King James I of England as a present.

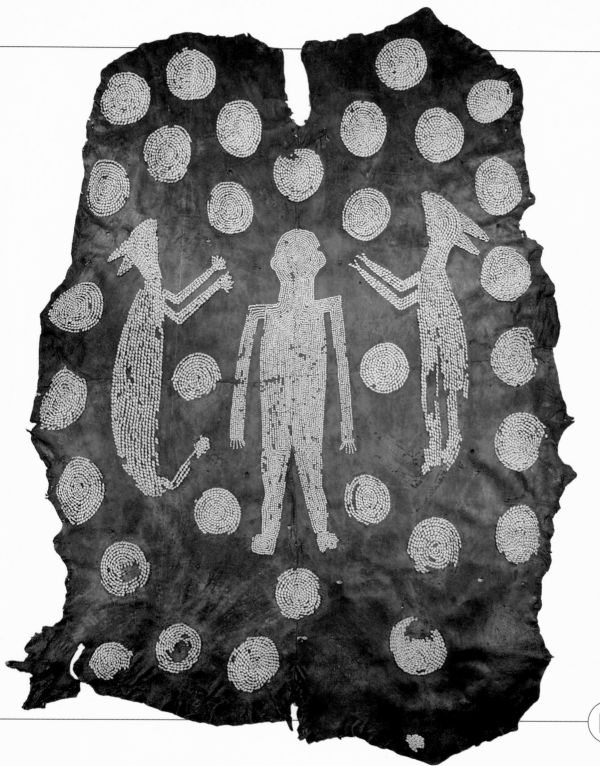

17

An English explorer named John White drew these pictures in 1585. They show life in **Native American** villages like the one Pocahontas lived in.

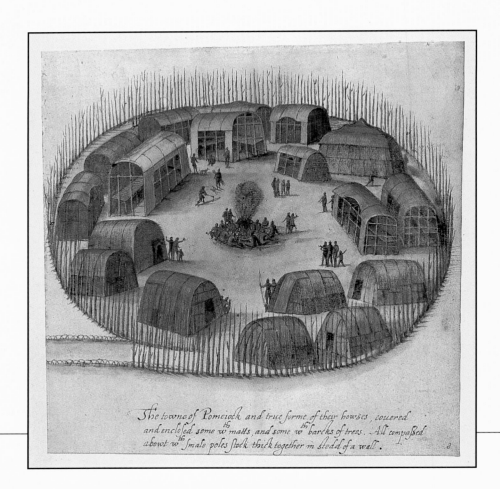

The towne of Pomeiock and true forme of their howses, couered and enclosed some wth matts, and some wth barcks of trees. All compaßed abowt wth smale poles stock thick together in stedd of a wall.

Builders used tree branches to make the shapes of the houses. Then they covered them with mats made from **reeds**.

We know what Pocahontas looked like.
These pictures of her were painted in
1616, when she visited England.

Ætatis suæ 21. Aº 1616.

This is a **portrait** of Pocahontas and her two-year-old son, Thomas Rolfe.

We know about Pocahontas's life because people wrote about it. This book was written by John Smith in 1624. It is called *The Generall Historie of Virginia, New England and the Summer Isles.*

You can find many **biographies** of
Pocahontas in your local library. You can
even learn about her in movies and on TV.

Glossary

artifact object made by people, usually from long ago

biography book that tells about a person's life

cloak coat with no sleeves

Native American another name for American Indians

portrait picture of a person

reed long grass with a hollow stem that grows near water

settler person who moves to a new place to live

tribe group of people who have the same leader, beliefs, and customs

warrior soldier

Index

More Books to Read

Adams, Patricia. *The Story of Pocahontas, Indian Princess.* Milwaukee: Gareth Stevens, 1996.

Benjamin, Anne. *Young Pocahontas: Indian Princess.* Mahwah, N.J.: Troll Communications, 1996.

Penner, Lucille R. *The True Story of Pocahontas.* New York: Random House, 1994.